Hot Springs Vacation

At the end of last year, I took a trip to the hot springs with a group of manga artists. "It is extremely difficult for busy people, especially manga artists, to coordinate anything as a group." (That's a line from Mikio Ito's *Normandy Secret Club.*) Normally, group trips like this one don't happen, but it did. We were loud on the bus ride there, enjoyed the hot springs, and relaxed at the inn. It was like being on a school trip again after 20 years. It lasted only two days and one night, but we all had a great time.

It's something that's not likely to happen every year, but if the opportunity arises, I would really like to go again.

—Nobuhiro Watsuki

Nobuhiro Watsuki earned international accolades for his first major manga series, **Rurouni Kenshin**, about a wandering swordsman in Meiji Era Japan. Serialized in Japan's *Weekly Shonen Jump* from 1994 to 1999, **Rurouni Kenshin**, available in North America from VIZ Media, quickly became a worldwide sensation, inspiring a spin-off short story ("Yahiko no Sakabatô"), an animated TV show and a series of novels. Watsuki's latest hit, **Buso Renkin**, began publication in *Weekly Shonen Jump* in 2003 and was adapted into an animated TV series in 2006.

BUSO RENKIN

VOL. 7

The SHONEN JUMP ADVANCED
Manga Edition

STORY AND ART BY
NOBUHIRO WATSUKI

English Adaptation/Lance Caselman
Translation/Toshifumi Yoshida
Touch-up Art & Lettering/James Gaubatz
Design/Yukiko Whitley
Editor/Amy Yu

Editor in Chief, Books/Alvin Lu
Editor in Chief, Magazines/Marc Weidenbaum
VP of Publishing Licensing/Rika Inouye
VP of Sales/Gonzalo Ferreyra
Sr. VP of Marketing/Liza Coppola
Publisher/Hyoe Narita

Printed in the U.S.A.

Published by VIZ Media, LLC
P.O. Box 77010
San Francisco, CA 94107

SHONEN JUMP ADVANCED Manga Edition
10 9 8 7 6 5 4 3
First printing, August 2007
Third printing, November 2007

www.viz.com

PARENTAL ADVISORY
BUSO RENKIN is rated T+ for Older Teen and is recommended for ages 16 and up. This volume contains fantasy violence.
ratings.viz.com

SHONEN JUMP ADVANCED MANGA EDITION

STORY & ART BY
NOBUHIRO WATSUKI

Vol. 7
Runaway Start

Alchemy
Alchemy is an early scientific practice combining elements of various disciplines that swept through Europe over the millennia. Its goals were the transmutation of base metals into gold and the creation of an Elixir of Immortality, neither of which succeeded. But unknown to the world at large, alchemy achieved two earthshaking supernatural successes–the homunculi and the kakugane.

Kazuki Muto

Kazuki was once killed by a homunculus but was restored to life by Tokiko, who replaced his heart with a magical talisman called a kakugane. Kazuki is 16 years old, a year older than his sister Mahiro. His Buso Renkin is a lance called "Sunlight Heart."

武装錬金

CHARACTERS

Homunculus
An artificial being created by alchemy. The form and powers of the homunculus differ depending on the organism it was based on. Homunculi feed on human flesh, and can only be destroyed by the power of alchemy.

Kakugane
The kakugane are forged from a magical alchemic alloy. They are activated by the deepest part of the human psyche, one's basic instincts. Each kakugane can materialize a unique weapon called a Buso Renkin.

Tokiko Tsumura

A girl chosen to be an Alchemist Warrior, an expert of Buso Renkin. Her Buso Renkin is a Death Scythe called the "Valkyrie Skirt."

Hiwatari
Captain Bravo (Mamoru Sakimori)
Papillon (Koushaku Chouno)
Chitose
Ouka Hayasaka
Angel Gozen

STORY

Alchemist Warrior Tokiko Tsumura comes to Ginsei City and uses herself as bait for the homunculi, artificial life forms that lurk in the darkness to devour unsuspecting humans. Unaware of Tokiko's intentions, high school student Kazuki Muto tries to save her and is killed in the process. Tokiko restores Kazuki's life with an alchemic talisman called a kakugane, and now he fights at Tokiko's side.
Kazuki and his fellow Alchemist Warriors are ordered to seek out and destroy the L.X.E., an evil organization of homunculi. L.X.E. leader Doctor Butterfly plans to revive a former Alchemist Warrior named Victor, so he plots to take the life energy of all the students at Ginsei Academy in order to do so.
Kazuki arrives too late to stop Victor's awakening and actually has his Buso Renkin, the Sunlight Heart, broken during battle. Since the kakugane was acting as Kazuki's heart as well, Kazuki seemingly dies. However, Kazuki's broken kakugane is actually a black kakugane (like the one Victor has), so Kazuki is endowed with great strength as well as skin and hair color like Victor. But the black kakugane makes Kazuki steal life energy from anyone around him, including all the students of the school. Seeing that the battle can't be settled right away, Victor leaves, claiming to want to see the world after a century of being dormant. With Victor gone, Kazuki's will to fight diminishes and he reverts to his normal self.
Summer vacation starts and the students of the dorm head to the beach for an overnight trip. That night, Captain Bravo tells Kazuki the history behind the black kakugane and Victor. He also reveals that Kazuki himself will become like Victor in six weeks and that an order has been placed by the Alchemist Army to re-exterminate Kazuki. Kazuki decides to fight, hoping to find a cure. Despite his resolve, Kazuki is defeated by Captain Bravo and is cast into the ocean. Tokiko recovers Kazuki from the sea and revives him, using her own life energy to do so. Kazuki and Tokiko decide to head for the place where Tokiko recovered the black kakugane. Seeing the bond between them, Gouta—a fellow Alchemist Warrior with feelings for Tokiko—leaves without a word...

Hideyuki Okakura
Masashi Daihama

Gouta Nakamura
Koji Rokumasu
Mahiro Muto
Saori Kawai
Chisato Wakamiya

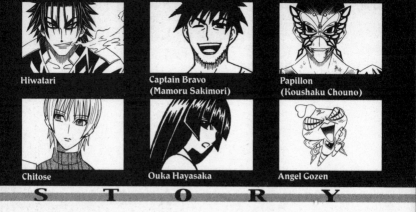

BUSO RENKIN
Volume 7: Runaway Start

CONTENTS

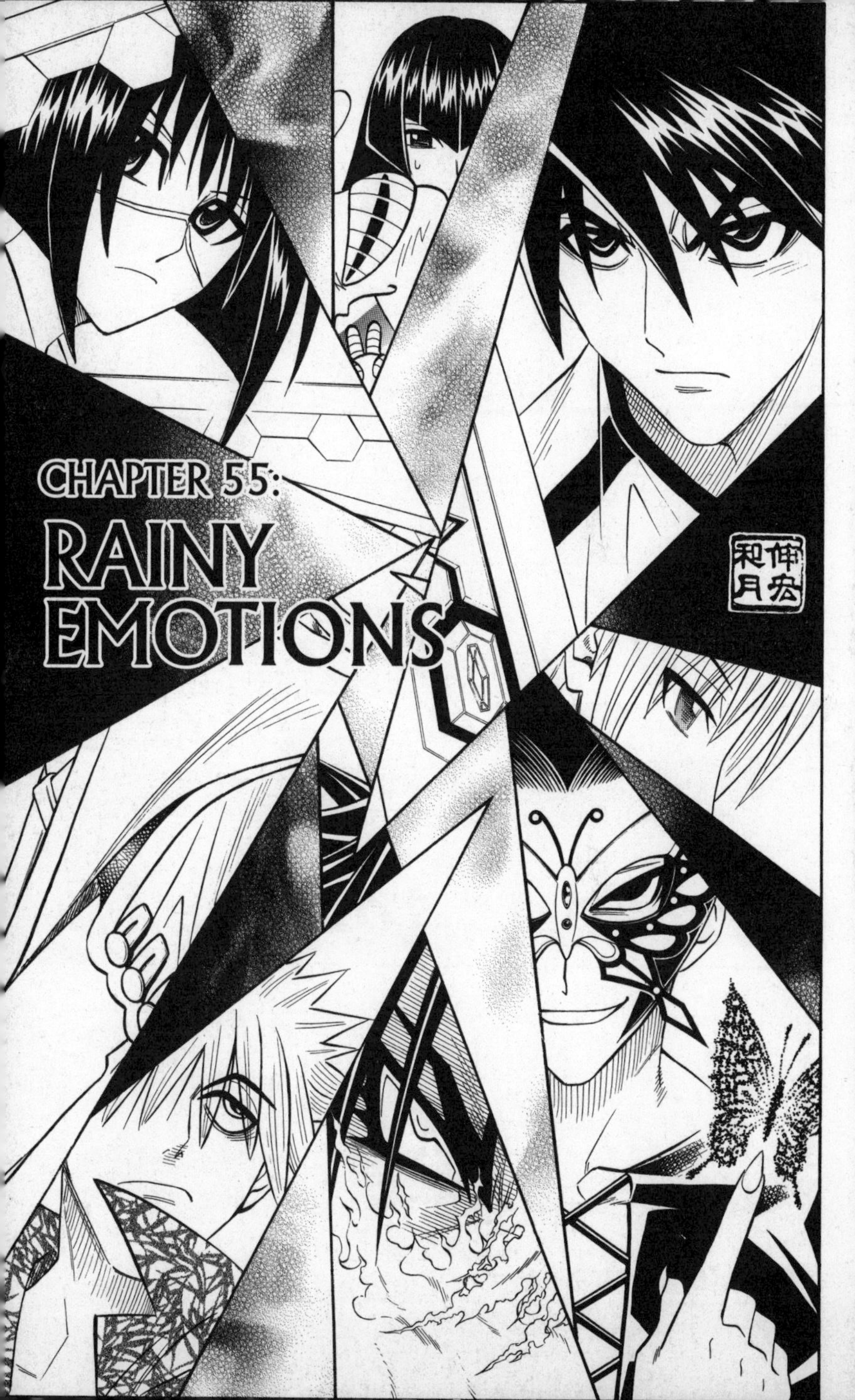
CHAPTER 55:
RAINY
EMOTIONS
伸宏
和月

WOI-NG

WAAAAAAAH!!

TWIRL.
WSP
TWIRL, TWIRL...
!!

WAAAAH!!
SW UP
GOOD MORNING.
WHAT ARE YOU GUYS DOING? IT'S STILL DARK OUT.
DOOOOM

KA-ZUKI! I'LL GET YOU!!
NO! IT WAS ALL ROKUMASU— UGH!
POW
WHAM
BAM
STOP THE ROUGH-HOUSING! PEOPLE ARE TRYING TO SLEEP!
SHEESH.
SHHK
GOOD, THEY'RE STILL ASLEEP.
LET'S SEE... MY BAGS ARE RIGHT ...
KLAK KLAK
... HERE.
TUG

BUSTED!
PLOOF
WE WERE JUST...
PRE-TENDING...
...TO BE ASLEEP.
GULP

WHERE'D YOU SNEAK OFF TO LAST NIGHT?
FWOOF
FWOOF
FWOOF
GETTING IN A LITTLE STRAWBERRY※ TIME?!
THAT'S A NO-NO! YOU MUST BE PUNISHED!
FWOOF
FWOOF

※ROMANCE

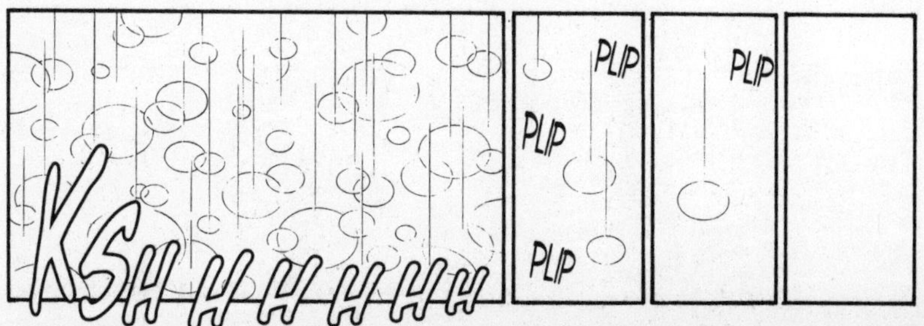

KSHHHH

GOING SOME-WHERE?

RIGHT NOW?

YEAH.

KSHHHH

WHERE YOU GOING AT THIS HOUR?

WE CAN'T SAY.

ANOTHER ONE OF YOUR "MISSIONS"?

SOMETHING LIKE THAT.

THEN I GUESS WE SHOULDN'T ASK QUESTIONS.

WE'D APPRECIATE IT.

BE CAREFUL.

GOOD LUCK, YOU GUYS!

TAKE THIS UMBRELLA. YOU CAN SHARE IT.

HAVE FUN!

OKAY, 'TIL NEXT SEMESTER THEN.
SEE YOU!
YEAH.
SEE YOU SOON!

...

THEIR WOUNDS HAVEN'T COMPLETELY HEALED.

NOPE.

KSHHHH

WE PRETENDED NOT TO NOTICE, BUT...

DID WE DO THE RIGHT THING?

You okay?

I THINK SO.

I'm fine.

AT LEAST THEY WON'T WORRY ABOUT WHAT WE'RE THINKING.

THE QUESTION IS, WHAT DO WE TELL BRAVO?
SHHK...
LET'S THINK ABOUT THAT OVER BREAKFAST.

KSHHHH
WHUP
LET'S GO, KAZUKI.
OKAY.
WE'LL BE BACK.
KRK
THAT'S A PROMISE!

KSHHHHHH
...
!
TUK
SPLAT
SPLOOSH
HEH
HEH HEH
HEH HEH HEH

WHAT ARE YOU LAUGHING AT?
GET UP, GOUTA.
IF YOU DON'T PASS SURVIVAL TRAINING...
TMP
HUFF
HUFF
HUFF
HUFF
...YOU'LL NEVER BECOME A WARRIOR.
I'M DONE.
HUFF
I CAN'T GO ON.
HUFF
HUFF
GET UP.
IF YOU DON'T, I CAN'T TREAT YOUR WOUNDS.

IF I REMEMBER RIGHT...
...YOUR WHOLE FAMILY WAS KILLED BY A HOMUNCULUS, RIGHT?
THAT'S RIGHT.
IS THAT WHAT HAPPENED TO YOU, TOKIKO?
SORT OF...
I ONLY KNOW WHAT I'VE BEEN TOLD.
TOLD?
I DON'T REMEMBER MUCH ABOUT IT.
THE DOCTORS SAY THE SHOCK GAVE ME PARTIAL AMNESIA.
BUT I REMEMBER THE FEAR.
AND THE HATE I FELT THEN IS STILL STRONG INSIDE OF ME.
I'M GOING TO KILL EVERY HOMUNCULUS I CAN FIND!
THAT'S WHY I'M HERE, TO GAIN THE STRENGTH I NEED TO DO THAT.
THEN I GUESS WE'RE DIFFERENT.

I DON'T REMEMBER ANYTHING.

I WAS JUST A BABY.

I DON'T EVEN REMEMBER MY FAMILY, MUCH LESS THE BEAST THAT KILLED THEM.

MY EARLIEST MEMORIES ARE OF AN ORPHANAGE RUN BY THE ALCHEMIST ARMY.

SOMEBODY THOUGHT I HAD THE POTENTIAL TO BE A WARRIOR, SO THAT'S WHY I'M HERE.

THAT'S IT, REALLY.

YOU'VE GOT SOMETHING TO FIGHT FOR.

I DON'T.

SO I GUESS...

...I'M THROUGH.

I SEE.

THEN YOU'LL BE SORRY YOU DIDN'T TOUGH IT OUT.

THIS IS YOUR CHANCE TO MAKE YOURSELF STRONG FOR THAT DAY.

NOW...

GET UP, GOUTA.

HER WORDS WERE WHAT KEPT ME GOING.
I WORKED HARD TO BECOME AN ALCHEMIST WARRIOR, BUT...
KS
H H H H
I'M DONE.
I CAN'T GO ON.
WHAP
HUH?!
ON YOUR FEET!

BINGO.
YOU'RE WARRIOR GOUTA.
HUH?

YOU DON'T KNOW WHO I AM, DO YOU?
EVER HEAR THE NAME "HIWATARI"?
FWOOSH

!!
HIWA-TARI ?!

THEY SAY HE'S A POWERFUL WARRIOR CHIEF!
WARRIOR CHIEF HIWA-TARI!!
DIDN'T SAKIMORI TEACH YOU ANYTHING?
NEVER MIND...
WHAT HAPPENED WITH YOUR MISSION?

WEREN'T YOU SUPPOSED TO DETAIN WARRIOR TOKIKO?
I DON'T SEE HER WITH YOU. DID YOU FAIL?
TWITCH
THEN ...

IS SHE...
...WITH KAZUKI MUTO RIGHT NOW?
TAKE ME TO THEM!
AS OF NOW, YOU'RE A MEMBER OF THE RE-EXTERMINATION SQUAD.
WE'RE GOING TO RE-EXTERMINATE KAZUKI MUTO, CODENAMED VICTOR III!
!
TOMP
WHAT IF YOU'RE THE ONLY THING STANDING BETWEEN THAT PERSON AND DEATH?
KRRK

AND THEN...
...WE'LL DEAL WITH...
...THAT TRAITOR TOKIKO AS WELL.
HOLD ON!
WE DON'T KNOW IF SHE REALLY BETRAYED US OR NOT!
SPLASH
SPLASH
WE SHOULD CAPTURE HER AND LET A COURT DECIDE WHAT TO DO WITH HER.
SHUDDER
YEAH, WE SHOULD.
THAT WOULD BE THE RIGHT THING TO DO.
BUT SOMETIMES IT'S MORE FUN...
...TO BREAK THE RULES.

SHEEN
SKREECH
SKREECH
HEY!
THUMP
CHAK
IT'S ABOUT TIME.
WHERE YOU MORONS BEEN?

NO. 5—NEGORO!

NO. 4—MARUYAMA!

NO. 6—INUKAI!

NO. 3—IKUSABE!

AND NO. 2—BUSUJIMA!

ALL THE MEMBERS...

...OF THE RE-EXTERMINATION SQUAD ARE PRESENT AND ACCOUNTED FOR!

KSHHHHHH
ALL RIGHT, HERE'S THE DEAL.
WE'RE GONNA DESTROY VICTOR III.
WHAT IF...
AND WE'VE GOT A TRAITOR TO DEAL WITH, TOO.
MAYBE WE CAN HAVE A LITTLE FUN WITH HER BEFORE WE KILL HER.
...YOU FIND SOMEONE...
...YOU WANT TO PROTECT?
WELL, WHAT ARE YOU WAITING FOR?
TAKE US TO THEM!
NO.
WHAT?

I DON'T CARE WHAT SHE DID!
THEN YOU'LL BE SORRY...
...YOU DIDN'T TOUGH IT OUT.
I WON'T HELP YOU KILL TOKIKO!
KRK
THIS IS YOUR CHANCE!...
...TO MAKE YOURSELF STRONG FOR THAT DAY.
I WON'T DO IT!!
FWASH
HAVE YOU LOST YOUR MIND?
IT'S SIX AGAINST ONE!!

The New Light that Shines Toward the Heavens!

Buso Renkin File No. 11

サンライトハート 改

SUNLIGHT HEART PLUS

SUNLIGHT HEART+

- Kakugane Serial Number: III (Black Kakugane)
- Creator: Kazuki Muto
- Form: Lance
- Main Colors: Silver-white, Bright Yellow, and Red
- Special Abilities:
  - At the will of the wielder, the energy in the lance activates, allowing the tip to separate and grow to any size necessary.
- Special Traits:
  - Very difficult to destroy with conventional attacks.
  - Since Sunlight Heart Plus acts as Kazuki Muto's heart, Kazuki cannot survive if it is removed or destroyed.
  - The lance is powered by Kazuki's own life-force. When he is in his "Victor" form, he involuntarily absorbs the life-forces of those around him, and the output of the lance is tremendously increased.
- Author's Notes:
  - The powering up of the main character's weapon is a staple of boy's manga, and I've been trying to think of a way to power up Kazuki's lance ever since the series started. The original Sunlight Heart was designed by a professional, but it was big and complicated, which made combat scenes a pain. This new design is a welcome change.
  - It looks more like a sword than a lance now, but I gave it the ability to grow and become like the old Sunlight Heart.
  - The basic design is more or less the same. I just kept my favorite features and simplified it. Of course, one should respect the work of a professional designer. To show my gratitude, I kept the dragon-face motif on the tip of the handle.

CHAPTER 56: THE NEW THIRD

CHAPTER 56: THE NEW THIRD

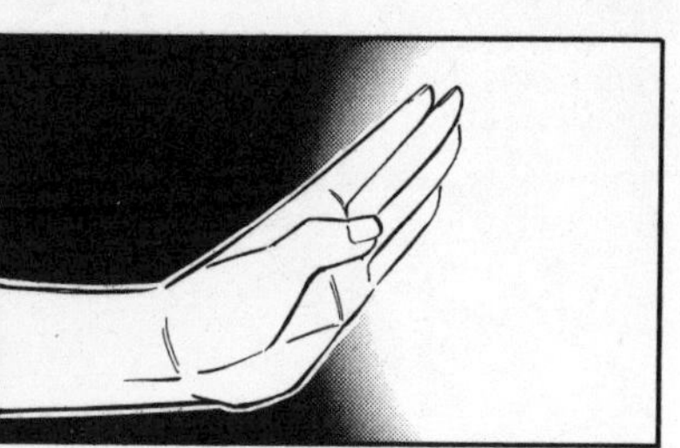

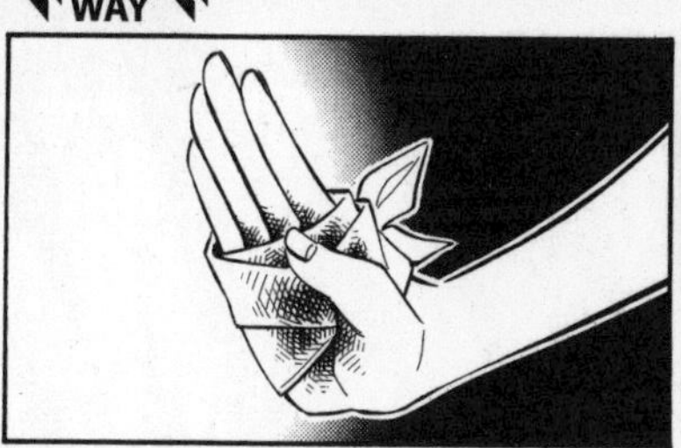

KRASH
!!!
KRASH
FWASH

BOOM
TUMP
THUD
FWOOSH...

REMOTE DETONATION ABILITY?
TELEKINESIS?
THWOOOOM

FWOOOOO
...

NO. YOU LAUNCHED SOME SMALL HIGH-SPEED MISSILES...
...THAT CIRCLED AROUND BEYOND OUR FIELD OF VISION TO STRIKE FROM THE SIDES.
HMPH

SHOOM
SHOOM

BUSO RENKIN OF THE CHAKRAM ...
MOTOR GEARS!
SHA-SHING
WHAT'S A CHAKRAM?
THEY'RE PROJECTILE WEAPONS FROM INDIA...
SORT OF LIKE SHURIKEN.

HE DESTROYED OUR VEHICLES AND SET UP A SMOKE SCREEN...
...SO THAT HE CAN ESCAPE.
CLEVER.
YES.
WARRIOR CHIEF HIWATARI, THE FIRE WILL DRAW A CROWD.
IF WE'RE GOING TO PLAY, WE SHOULD GET TO IT.

DON'T TELL ME WHAT TO DO!
I'LL MURDER YOU!
WHHRRR
WIP
!
FIRST YOU LAUNCH A SNEAK ATTACK...
...THEN YOU STAND THERE FACING ME LIKE WE'RE IN DODGE CITY?
ALL RIGHT!!
FWOOM

WRRR

HE'LL USE THE CHAKRAM TO ESCAPE.

AS SOON AS HE THROWS THEM, HE'LL MAKE A RUN FOR IT THROUGH THE SMOKE.

WELL, IF HE KNOWS ANYTHING ABOUT HIWATARI, THAT'S NOT A BAD IDEA.

WE CAN'T LET HIM GET AWAY.

THE FIRE TRUCKS ARE THREE MILES AWAY. THEY'LL BE HERE IN TEN MINUTES.

FWRRR

I'LL DO THE COUNTDOWN.

THREE ...

TWO ...

ONE.

BOOOM

GRAAH!!
GO!!
TMP
FWOOSH
HE'S RUNNING.
HUH?!
WHAT?!

SKROSHHHHHOOM
...SKY WALKER MODE!!
MOTOR GEARS...
IT'S THE LEADER I WANT!!
IF I TAKE HIM OUT, I CAN PROTECT TOKIKO!!
GWAAAAH!!!

GOT 'IM!
NOT QUITE.
?!
FWASH

FWOOM
GAAH!!
SPLOOSH
HMPH.
THE OCEAN ...
FWOOOOOO

ARE YOU ALL RIGHT?
THAT PUNK!
HE CAN'T GET AWAY!
TMP
FWOOOO
THAT'S IT FOR NOW. WE CAN'T STAY HERE.
BESIDES...
...THE ENEMY HAS FLED THE BATTLEFIELD.
GLUP
GLUP
VWRRRRRR
MOTOR GEARS...
...MARINE DIVER MODE!
THAT BLOW SHOULD'VE DISABLED HIM, BUT HE WASN'T EVEN FAZED!
HE'S NOT JUST A PYROKINETIC...

WHAT KIND OF BUSO RENKIN DOES HE HAVE?!

HE WASN'T TRYING TO GET AWAY.

HE STARTED THE FIRE TO ATTRACT PEOPLE SO THAT WE'D HAVE TO CUT SHORT OUR BATTLE.

KSHHHHH

THEN HE WENT FOR OUR LEADER. HE WAS WILLING TO DIE TO TAKE HIM OUT.

HE KNOWS HOW TO USE HIS BUSO RENKIN, TOO.

PROPERLY TRAINED, HE'D MAKE A GOOD WARRIOR.

!
THOSE ROCKS...
THAT'S WHERE I FOUGHT BRAVO LAST NIGHT.
THAT'S WHERE WE PARTED WAYS.
KSHHHHH
I NEVER THOUGHT WE'D END UP IN A SITUATION LIKE THIS.
IT'S HARD TO BELIEVE.
YOU AND BRAVO ARE MY COMRADES IN ARMS.
I JUST WANT THE THREE OF US TO GET STARTED ON A NEW MISSION.
NOW IT'S JUST US.
YEAH.
I GUESS WE'LL HAVE TO GET USED TO FIGHTING AS A DUO.

HAAH !!

HAAH !!

SPLASH

!!!

The Gears of Wisdom Spin at High-Speed!

Buso Renkin File No. 12

MOTOR GEARS

- Kakugane Serial Number: LV (55)
- Creator: Gouta Nakamura
- Form: Chakram
- Main Colors: Gold and Indigo
- Special Abilities: · Velocity, angle of attack, and RPM can be programmed before they are thrown. They can also be used as hand weapons.
- Special Traits:
  - Programming is done through neural induction.
  - Their power source is the body's motor impulses. When thrown, they run on internal power storage. Consequently, this Buso Renkin has one of the lowest power profiles.
  - The Chakram can also be attached to the hands and feet and used in the following ways:
    On the fists: Knuckle Duster Mode (increased impact damage)
    On the ankles: Sky Walker Mode (increased speed and mobility)
    On the soles of the feet: Marine Diver Mode (increased mobility in water)
- Author's Notes:
  - The Motor Gears were inspired by a large gear that I found as a child. I was really excited because it looked like a weapon or some kind of secret key. I even hid it so that no one would find it. But before long, I lost it.
  - Kazuki is the embodiment of power and determination while Tokiko embodies speed and berserk rage. It occurred to me that a small, versatile Buso Renkin would complement their more powerful weaponry. Gouta turned out better than I'd hoped.
  - The design is a circle and a hexagon. I decided that simplicity was best in this case. Their geometric forms are really cool.
  - I had a hard time coming up with a name for this. The chakram is a weapon from India so I researched names of Indian gods and heroes, but nothing really grabbed me. As the deadline loomed, I got desperate and blurted out, "They're gears that run on the body's motor impulses, so they're Motor Gears!" and that was that. In retrospect, I think that name works pretty well since not many people know what a chakram is anyway.

I SEE...
FWOOOO
WARRIOR CHIEF HIWATARI...
...AND THE RE-EXTERMINATION SQUAD...
SO NOW WE'RE UP AGAINST...
...TWO WARRIOR CHIEFS AND FIVE WARRIORS.
KSH
IF WE GO AT THEM HEAD ON...
HHH
HHH
...
WELL, I DON'T EVEN WANT TO THINK ABOUT THAT.
YEAH, AND WE DON'T WANT TO BURN DOWN THE CITY, EITHER.
SORRY.
MY BAD.
I HAVE A FEELING...
...THAT BEING ON THE RUN...
...IS REALLY GONNA SUCK.
WOOOOOO

CHAPTER 57: RUNAWAY START

CHAPTER 57: RUNAWAY START

KSHHHH
GOUTA...
...YOU SHOULD GO TO HQ AND TURN YOURSELF IN.
YOU'LL STILL HAVE TO FACE DISCIPLINARY ACTION...
...BUT AT LEAST YOU WON'T GET KILLED.
HHHH
NO.
I'M COMING WITH YOU.
WE'RE IN THIS TOGETHER.
THE RE-EXTERMI-NATION SQUAD HAS ALREADY...
...PUT TOKIKO ON THEIR HIT LIST.
IT'S A DONE DEAL.
I'M COMING WITH YOU.
TMP

KAZUKI MUTO...
THIS IS ALL...
...YOUR FAULT!

SWAK

...

OWW!!
ZING
ZING
ZING
ZING
STOP IT, YOU TWO!!

I'D BETTER DRESS THAT FOR YOU.
TMP TMP TMP
HUH?
IT'S OKAY. I ALREADY ...
NO.
I WENT TOO FAR LAST NIGHT.
I'M SORRY.

...

LOOKS LIKE WE BOTH HURT THE SAME HAND.

ANYWAY ... WHADDAYA SAY?

...

WAH WAH WAH WAH

TWO VEHICLES AND...

...ONE ABANDONED BUILDING WERE INCINERATED.

FWRRR

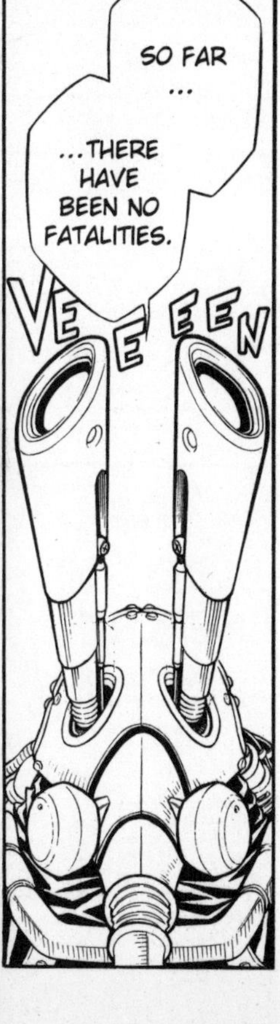

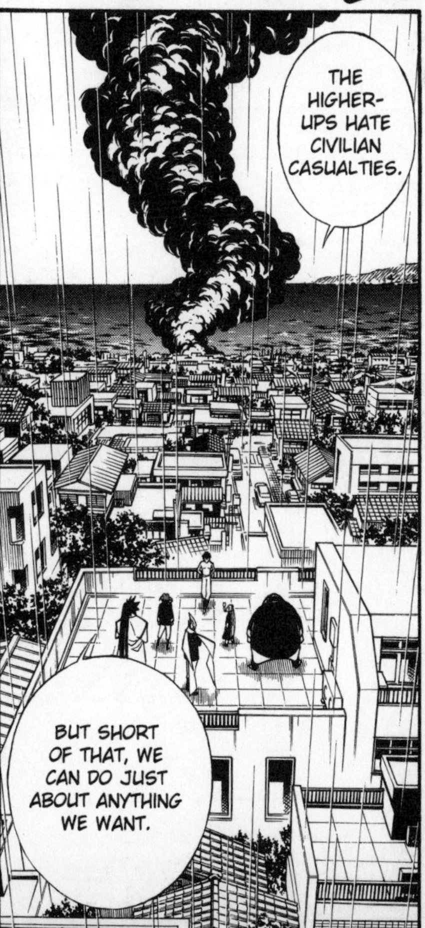

A DIRTY RAG?

I RECOVERED IT FROM THE BATTLE ZONE.

IT'S THE HANDKERCHIEF THE ROOKIE HAD WRAPPED AROUND HIS HAND.

EXCELLENT.

MY BUSO RENKIN CAN TRACK HIM FROM THAT.

AND MY BUSO RENKIN...

...CAN SET UP AN AMBUSH.

WARRIOR CHIEF...
WHAT NOW?
DO YOU HAVE TO ASK?
YOU KNOW HOW I ROLL.

LIKE I ALWAYS SAY...

...THE FASTEST CAT GETS THE TASTIEST PARTS.

KRAK

KRAK

SRIP
KRAK
YOU'RE BEING IRRATIONAL, AS ALWAYS.
YOU HAVE NO PLAN AT ALL.
...
WELL? WHAT ABOUT YOU?

THAT'S RIGHT.

HEY, OUR BATTLE FOR SUPREMACY IS POWERED BY ALCHEMY, REMEMBER? IN AN IRRATIONAL WORLD...

...WHAT GOOD IS RATIONALITY?

AND DON'T FORGET, OUR TARGET THIS TIME...

...EVEN IF HE HASN'T FULLY TRANS-FORMED...

...IS A "VICTOR" WITH A BLACK KAKU-GANE.

AN IRRATIONAL SITUATION CALLS FOR AN IRRATIONAL APPROACH.

THAT'S ME ALL THE WAY!

KS
HHHHHH
旅館
三浦屋
SO...
...THEY WENT TO A VILLAGE TO GROW SOME STRAWBERRIES.
ACTUALLY, THEY WENT TO PICK SOME STRAWBERRIES!
NO WAY. THEY ACTUALLY WENT TO LOOK FOR THE LEGENDARY "LOST STRAWBERRY."
I THINK THEY REALLY JUST WANTED TO BE ALONE AND MAKE STRAWBERRY-TIME FOR THE REST OF THE SUMMER.
COMBAT
WVRRRRR
BEEP
KS
HHH
HELLO ... SAKIMORI?
THAT'S RIGHT.
I JUST GOT WORD FROM HEAD-QUARTERS.
!
KAZUKI MUTO...
...IS STILL ALIVE!

HE KNOWS WE'RE LYING!

YOU DON'T THINK HE'S BUYING THE STRAWBERRY STORY?

YACK

I JUST FOUND OUT MYSELF.

YACK

WHAT IF WE TELL HIM THEY'RE ON A TRIP TO HAWAII?

AAAAAH!!!

I'LL DROP THE KIDS OFF AND COME AT ONCE.

...

YOU SOUND RELIEVED.

HUH?

DON'T PLAY DUMB.

YOUR HEART'S NOT IN THIS. I CAN HEAR IT IN YOUR VOICE.

DON'T FORGET ...

WE WERE PARTNERS ONCE.

BEEP

HONESTLY!

I EXPECTED BETTER FROM THE BOTH OF YOU!

YOU'RE ACTING LIKE CHILDREN!

I'M GOING TO WITHDRAW MONEY FROM THE ATM BEFORE THEY FREEZE MY ACCOUNT. WAIT HERE.

SPLISH

SPLISH

KSHHHH

JUST SO YOU KNOW, I'M NOT DOING THIS FOR YOU.

THE TRUTH IS...

...I DON'T CARE WHAT HAPPENS TO YOU.

TOKIKO'S THE ONLY ONE I CARE ABOUT!!
AND I DON'T CARE WHAT HAPPENS TO ME, EITHER!
YOU KNOW ...
I THINK I'M GOING TO GET ALONG WITH YOU JUST FINE.

OKAY!

GOUTA, STOP PUSHING!

WANT TO BUY ANOTHER UMBRELLA?

NO! ER.. IT'S A WASTE OF MONEY.

LET'S GO!!

I THOUGHT SO.
KRASH

THE ALCHEMIST ARMY MAY KNOW ABOUT THE BLACK KAKUGANE, BUT...
TUP
TUP
...I KNOW FAR MORE ABOUT MUTO THAN THEY DO.

HE WON'T BE EASY TO KILL...

...AND HE'LL NEVER GIVE UP.

ESTIMATED TIME UNTIL KAZUKI MUTO PERMANENTLY TRANSFORMS INTO A VICTOR:

— 41 DAYS —

- Height: 175 cm; Weight: 63 kg
- Born: April 19; Aries; Blood Type: AB; Age: 17
- Likes: Tokiko Tsumura, turquoise blue color, Hawaiian shirts
- Dislikes: Junk food, enemies of Tokiko
- Hobby: All kinds of aquatic sports
- Special Ability: He can do anything for Tokiko
- Affiliations: Alchemist Army, Warrior (Rookie)

Character File No. 27

GOUTA NAKAMURA

Author's Notes

- Gouta was originally supposed to be the sidekick of the main character of my series, *Gun Blaze West*. His main theme was supposed to be "love."
- I had a rough idea for this character even before I started this series. Originally, he was supposed to be a student at Ginsei Academy who becomes an Alchemist Warrior like Kazuki. I was going to have him be in love with Mahiro instead of Tokiko. But things change and with all of last year's work, he ended up being the way he is now.
- Gouta is very much a realist. The only fantasy in his life is Tokiko. He will remain loyal and devoted to her no matter what happens. A character whose sole motivation is the love of a girl is new for me, but I really enjoy drawing him. He's become one of my favorite characters.
- I really don't think his chances with Tokiko are very good, but maybe they can at least be good friends.

CHAPTER 58:
EPISODE ZERO

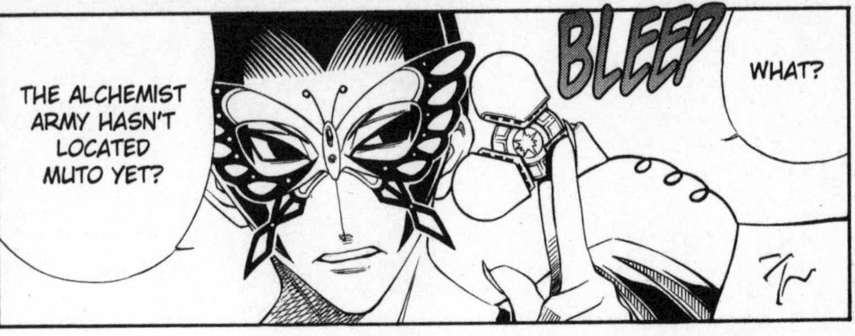

I WONDER WHERE KAZUKI IS.

HE SHOULD BE BRAVE AND FACE HIS ENEMIES BOLDLY.

AND YOU SHOULD TRY TO BE LESS CONSPIC-UOUS!

IT SEEMS THAT KAZUKI, OR MORE LIKELY TOKIKO...
...IS AVOIDING PLACES WHERE THE ALCHEMIST ARMY MIGHT LOOK.
AND THEIR PURSUERS...

...THIS RE-EXTERMINATION SQUAD...
...SOUND VERY DANGEROUS. SO BE CAREFUL.

IF I WERE TO DESCRIBE THEM WITH A SINGLE WORD, IT WOULD BE...

...*MERCENARY.*

THEY'RE EXTREMELY SKILLED, BUT THEY ALL SEEM TO HAVE DIFFICULTY FITTING IN.

SO THEY'VE BEEN GROUPED TOGETHER UNDER A WARRIOR CHIEF THAT CAN CONTROL THEM—THROUGH FORCE, IF NECESSARY. THAT'S THE *RE-EXTERMINATION SQUAD!*

BUT WHY DID THEY SEND THESE SCARY GUYS AFTER KAZUKI AND TOKIKO?

THE ALCHEMIST ARMY CONSIDERS THE UPCOMING BATTLE WITH VICTOR THE FOREMOST CONCERN. IT'S PREPARING MOST OF ITS FORCES TO FACE HIM.

THE RE-EXTERMINATION SQUAD WAS THE ONLY TEAM AVAILABLE...

THE MAN WHO KNOWS KAZUKI BEST...
THE ONLY ONE WHO HAS A BUSO RENKIN THAT CAN COUNTER THE ENERGY DRAIN...
CAPTAIN BRAVO.
THE RE-EXTERMINATION SQUAD, CAPTAIN BRAVO, ETC....
THEY MEAN NOTHING TO ME.
I JUST WANT TO KNOW WHERE MUTO IS, AND...
...WHERE HE'S GOING!
I DON'T BELIEVE THEY'RE WANDERING AIMLESSLY.
THEY'RE HEADED SOMEWHERE.
I AGREE.
I'LL SEE WHAT I CAN FIND OUT.

AND I'LL KEEP...
WAAH
FLASH
WAAH
FLASH
I SAID, LESS CONSPIC-UOUS!!
WAAH
WAAH

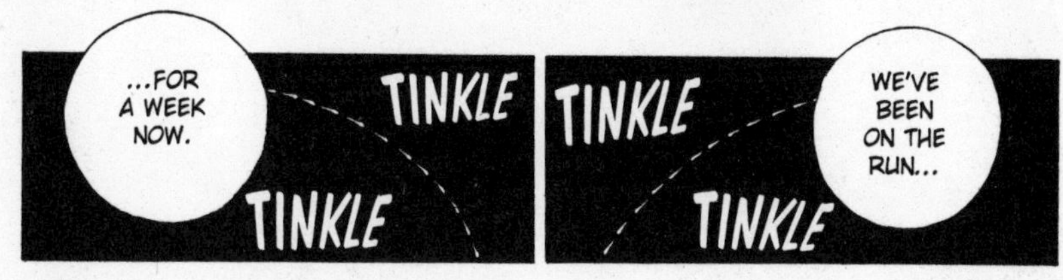
WE'VE BEEN ON THE RUN...
TINKLE
TINKLE
TINKLE
TINKLE
...FOR A WEEK NOW.

WHERE ARE WE?
NO IDEA.
ASK TOKIKO.

UNDER-DOG!!
PEEK

LOOK! I CAN PEE FARTHER THAN YOU!
SPLEESH
STOP POLLUTING THE RIVER!
AND DO YOUR BUSINESS WHERE I CAN'T SEE YOU!

HONESTLY...
WHAT ARE YOU TWO? FIVE?
WELL, I THINK...
...WE'RE GETTING ALONG BETTER THAN WE WERE.

SHAKE!
WIP
BACK OFF!
YOU HAVEN'T CHANGED AT ALL.
AND WASH YOUR HANDS FIRST!

C'MON, GOUTA.
CAN'T YOU AT LEAST TRY TO GET ALONG WITH KAZUKI?
NOT POSSIBLE.
I JUST DON'T LIKE THAT GUY.
ONE OF THESE DAYS, I'M GOING TO BEAT HIM AND MAKE HIM CRY UNCLE.
UNCLE.

COME HERE! I'LL MAKE *YOU* CRY UNCLE!!
TMP TMP TMP
SO, TOKIKO...
WHERE ARE WE?
THE TOWN OF OKUTAMA IN TOKYO?
THAT'S RIGHT. AFTER WE LEFT CHIBA, WE SKIRTED THE POPULATED AREAS...
...CUT THROUGH NORTHERN SAITAMA, AND HERE WE ARE.
I CHOSE A ROUTE THAT WOULD BE HARD FOR ANYONE TO FOLLOW, BUT...
...ONCE WE LEAVE THESE WOODS, WE'LL BE EXPOSED UNTIL WE REACH OUR DESTINATION.
OUR DESTINATION...
THE PLACE WHERE YOU GOT THIS.

YES.
I SUPPOSE IT'S ABOUT TIME...
...THAT I TOLD YOU WHAT HAPPENED THERE.

TMP
LXX
WHISH
WOMP

TOMP
...
A FAKE.
THERE'S A LEGEND ABOUT THIS SCHOOL THAT DATES BACK FROM THE MEIJI ERA...
...OF A MIRACULOUS HEALING STONE.
IT'S BEEN CONFIRMED THAT THE STONE IS REALLY A KAKUGANE, BUT...
...WHERE'S THE REAL ONE?
WHUP
KLAK
KLAK
KLAK
KLAK
KLUNK

KRASSH

A BASEMENT.

KLAK KLAK

NO...

MORE LIKE AN UNDERGROUND CHAMBER.

TMP

ARE YOU...
...AN ALCHEMIST WARRIOR?
WHO'S THERE?!

KREESH
WHAP
TMP
TAKE IT. IT BELONGS TO YOU, ANYWAY.
USE IT IF YOU WANT, BUT WHATEVER HAPPENS, LET NO HARM COME TO IT.
FOR IF YOU DO...
...A TERRIBLE FATE WILL BEFALL YOU.

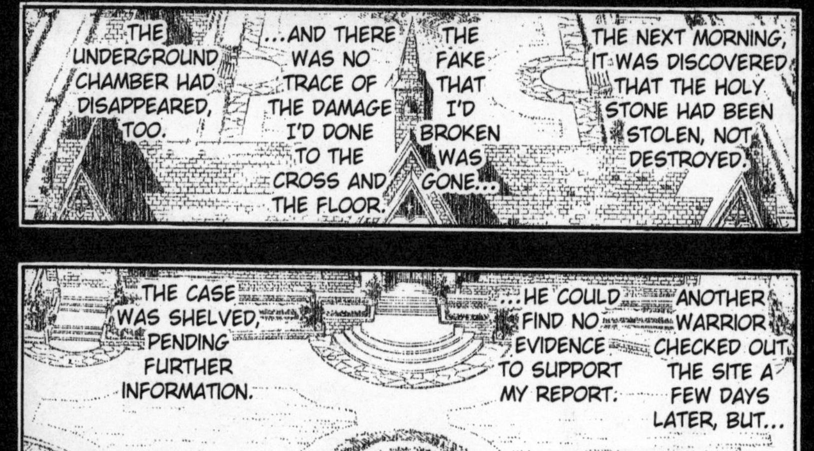
THE NEXT MORNING, IT WAS DISCOVERED THAT THE HOLY STONE HAD BEEN STOLEN, NOT DESTROYED.
THE FAKE THAT I'D BROKEN WAS GONE...
...AND THERE WAS NO TRACE OF THE DAMAGE I'D DONE TO THE CROSS AND THE FLOOR.
THE UNDERGROUND CHAMBER HAD DISAPPEARED, TOO.

ANOTHER WARRIOR CHECKED OUT THE SITE A FEW DAYS LATER, BUT...
...HE COULD FIND NO EVIDENCE TO SUPPORT MY REPORT.
THE CASE WAS SHELVED, PENDING FURTHER INFORMATION.

BUT I'M SURE OF IT! THE MAN IN THE MASK...
...KNOWS THINGS ABOUT THE BLACK KAKUGANE THAT'S IN KAZUKI!

HEAD-QUARTERS IS BUSY PREPARING FOR THE BATTLE AGAINST VICTOR...
...AND I DOUBT THE RE-EXTERMINATION SQUAD WOULD THINK TO CHECK OUT A LEAD LIKE THIS.
WE SHOULD GO STRAIGHT TO THE ACADEMY, AND...
...FIND THE MAN IN THE MASK!!

WHEN WE LEAVE OKUTAMA, WE'LL HEAD FOR YOKOHAMA.
THIS MAY BE THE LAST NIGHT WE CAN GET A GOOD NIGHT'S SLEEP FOR A WHILE.
SO GET PLENTY OF REST.

NEWTON APPLE ACADEMY FOR GIRLS?

YES.
THERE WERE SOME UNEXPLAINED DETAILS ABOUT THE INITIAL REPORT OF THE BLACK KAKUGANE'S RECOVERY.
NOT INTER-ESTED.
BUT...
YOU GO CHECK IT OUT IF YOU WANT.
THAT KIND OF THING'S RIGHT UP YOUR ALLEY.
BEE-BEE-BEEP
!

HEY...
YOU'D BETTER HURRY.
HUH?
IN A LITTLE WHILE, IT'S NOT GONNA MATTER ANYWAYS.
P251iS
From Number 6 Inukai
Subject Target Found
Date August X

LOOKS LIKE I'M THE FIRST ONE HERE.
WE HAVE TO BE ON THE MOVE BY 3:00, OKAY?
YEAH.
SOUNDS KINDA FUN, IN A WAY.
HE SAID...

Buso Renkin
ブソウレンキン

CHAPTER 59: NO INTENTION OF LOSING
MIDNIGHT
...
AM 0:00
IT'S TIME.
TMP
TUP
ZOOOM

CHAPTER 59:
NO INTENTION OF LOSING

KROOOSH
GRRRRR
TMP
EASY, BOYS ...
SAVE A LITTLE SOMETHING FOR ME.
KRUK

!
BUSO RENKIN ...
...OF THE MILITARY DOGS!
CRAP!
THEY SNIFFED US OUT!!
SHWOOSH
YOU MUST BE FROM THE RE-EXTERMINATION SQUAD!
YOU'VE GOT GUTS TO COME AFTER US BY YOURSELF!
THE TENTS WERE DECOYS, EH?
INTERESTING! THIS IS HOW I LIKE—

...
IF THIS IS A GAME TO YOU, THEN LEAVE.

THOOM
BECAUSE TO ME...
...THIS IS LIFE OR DEATH.
IF I DON'T KEEP MOVING FORWARD...
...MY LIFE...
...AND PROBABLY THOSE OF MY FRIENDS, IS OVER.

I'M NOT GOING TO MAKE TROUBLE FOR THE ALCHEMIST ARMY OR ENDANGER THE GENERAL POPULATION.
VREEEEE
BEFORE I BECOME A MONSTER FOR GOOD...
...I'LL FINISH MYSELF.
SO...
...LEAVE.
LOOKS LIKE YOU HAVE YOUR HANDS FULL...
TMP
...INUKAI.
!

I'M HERE TO HELP YOU.

BE GRATEFUL.

TMP

MARU-YAMA!

YOU FOLLOWED ME!

THUD

WOOSH

I WON'T ASK YOU TO LEAVE.

IF IT'S TROUBLE YOU WANT...

...I'LL GIVE YOU A BELLYFUL!

SHINK
I'LL SPLAT-TER
...
YOUR GUTS!!
...

HERE YOU GO!

HUH?!

DOOM
HEH HEH HEH
HEH HEH
HEH HEH
HEH HEH HEH
WHAT ARE THEY?
IS THIS HIS...
...BUSO RENKIN?

EXACTLY.
THWOOOO
THE BUSO RENKIN OF THE FLOATING MINES...
TINK
BUBBLE CAGE!
HEH HEH!
FWASH
BOOM
!
?!
SHRINK

WHAT HAPPENED?
FSSSSS
THE BALLOON MINES' BLASTS...
...SHRINK WHAT-EVER THEY TOUCH.
YOU'LL LOSE ABOUT SIX INCHES PER BLAST.
YOU'RE ABOUT FIVE FEET TALL, SO...
TEN MORE MINES AND YOU'RE HISTORY!
TOKIKO!
TOKI-KO!
NOW!
WHOOM
!

WHUP
FSSSSS
FSSSSS
DSHHHHH
BLUP
BLUP
KRAKEL
KRAKEL
CHANK
CHANK
WHY SHOULD I?!
LEAVE IF THIS IS A GAME TO ME?

DO YOU REALIZE WHAT DEFEATING YOU WILL DO FOR ME?
I'LL GET TO TAKE PART IN THE REAL SHOW, THE BATTLE AGAINST VICTOR!
GRAB
ATTACK, MY BUSO RENKIN OF THE MILITARY DOGS!!
KILLER RABIES!

THW
AM

I DON'T CARE WHO YOU ARE.

I HAVE NO INTENTION OF LOSING!

Buso Renkin
ブソウレンキン

CHAPTER 60: WIND AND LEAVES

SWIP
GIVE IT UP.
WHAT POWER...
AND HE DIDN'T EVEN TURN INTO A VICTOR.
...
IMPRESSIVE.

WOOOOOOOO
HMM...
YOU'RE NOT BAD, KID.
STILL...
WE HAVE NO INTENTION OF GIVING UP.
YOU HAVEN'T EVEN SEEN WHAT INUKAI'S KILLER RABIES CAN DO.
WHAT?!
BUT YOU REALLY SHOULD WORRY ABOUT YOUR OWN PROBLEMS.
OTHERWISE ...
HEE
HEE
HEE
HEE
!

!!
WHAT'S GOING ON?
FWASH
WAIT!
NORMALLY AFTER TAKING THAT KIND OF DAMAGE...
...A BUSO RENKIN TURNS BACK INTO A KAKUGANE.
AH!!
WHAM
WHAM

READ THIS WAY

PLURT

GOUTA!

GIVE UP, YOU SAY?

WE'RE JUST GETTING STARTED!

NOW YOU'LL SEE THE POWER OF...

...KILLER RABIES!

YOU'VE HEARD OF RABIES, HAVEN'T YOU?!
IT MAKES DOGS GO MAD!
AND THAT'S WHAT THEIR DEFAULT FORM IS— *MAD DOGS!*
I JUST RELEASED THE SAFETY LOCKS!
EVEN I CAN'T STOP THEM NOW!
THEY'LL KEEP ATTACKING UNTIL THEY'VE TORN EVERYONE IN THE AREA TO PIECES— EXCEPT FOR THE PERSON HOLDING THIS DOG WHISTLE!
NO-THING CAN STOP THEM NOW!!
UNH!!

!!!
SH
UNK
AGH!

CHOPPING THEM IN TWO ONLY WORKED AGAINST YOU!

WITH THEIR WEIGHT HALVED, THEIR SPEED IS DOUBLED!

STAND BACK!

YOUR LANCE IS TOO SLOW FOR THESE GUYS!

BUT YOUR CHAKRAM ISN'T POWERFUL ENOUGH TO TAKE THEM OUT.

WANT TO GIVE UP?
HA HA HA
DO YOU?
WELL, TOO BAD!
YOU'RE BOTH DEAD, AND SO IS THE WARRIOR GIRL!!
!

DO
OM

HEE
I AM ABLE TO MANEUVER MY BALLOON MINES, ALBEIT SLOWLY.
HEE
SORRY I DIDN'T EXPLAIN BEFORE.

IT'S ALL RIGHT.
KNOWING THAT THEY'RE BALLOONS IS ENOUGH.

THEY MAY BE BOMBS, BUT IF THEY'RE BALLOONS ...
FWOOSH
...THEN I CAN DO THIS!

I CAN CREATE A BLAST OF WIND...
...AND MOVE THEM WITHOUT TOUCHING THEM!!
SHOO
HEH
HEH
HEH
HEH
HA!

I'M SURPRISED. YOU DISCOVERED MY WEAKNESS AFTER ONLY BEING HIT ONCE.
AND YOU STRUCK BACK SO QUICKLY...
!
BUT IF ONE USES ONE'S WEAKNESS WISELY...
WOO
...IT CAN BECOME A STRENGTH.
SWO
?!
WITH YOUR BLADES STUCK IN MY BODY, YOUR OWN MOBILITY IS LIMITED.
NOW OPEN WIDE!
KA-BOOM
WIND!

BA-BA-BOOM
BA-BOOM
SHHRIIINK
TOKIKO! NO!

STRIKE, KILLER RABIES!
WHOOOO
THWIIIIIIING
SHOOOOSH
SHOOOOSH

WOOOOOOOOOOO
?!
HE'S USING THE LEAVES TO CAMOUFLAGE THE MOTOR GEARS...
BUT...
KILLER RABIES' SENSE OF SMELL IS KEENER THAN A BLOODHOUND'S!
SNIFF
THEY DON'T NEED TO SEE THEIR TARGET!!

SHUK
?!
NO! THE CHAKRAM WAS A DIVER-SION!!

THE LANCE WAS A DIVERSION, TOO.

PLUP

YOU'RE HALF RIGHT.

THE QUICKEST WAY TO TAKE OUT A REMOTE CONTROLLED BUSO RENKIN...

...IS TO TAKE OUT THE CONTROLLER.

YOU SAID...

...THE ONLY ONE WHO'S SAFE FROM ATTACK...

...IS THE ONE HOLDING THIS WHISTLE, RIGHT?

!!

TOKIKO!
FTCH
FTCH
TMP TMP TMP
TOKI-KO!
TO--
!!!

Beware of Mad Dogs!

Buso Renkin File No. 13

キラー
レイビーズ
KILLER RABIES

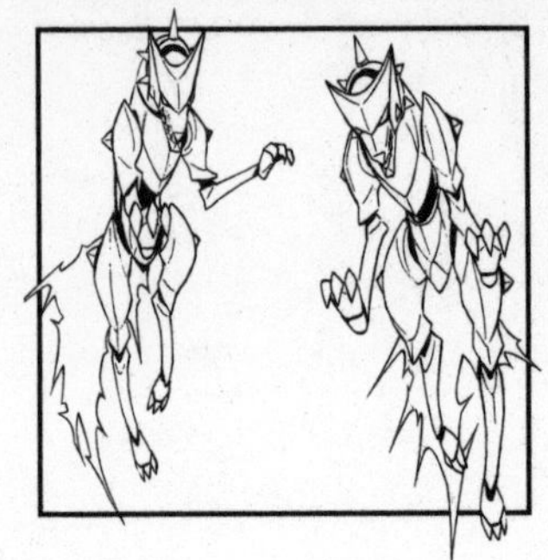

○ Kakugane Serial Number: XCII (92)

○ Creator: Rintaro Inukai

○ Form: Military Dogs

○ Main Colors: Magenta and Periwinkle

○ Special Abilities: · Automated mechanical attack dogs

○ Special Traits:
- They track their prey by scent, capture, and kill with claws and fangs.
- Intelligence is equal to a normal dog; their sense of smell is twice as good, and they are about ten times faster.
- In their default operating mode, they behave like rabid dogs. Inukai controls them with a special dog whistle via their special collar locks.

○ Author's Notes:
- I had the idea for a military dog Buso Renkin for a long time. Most people think that buso means "weapon," but I consider it to mean anything related to combat.
- Originally, I was thinking of having this be a bio-weapon that emitted a virus with rabies-like effects, but it would have caused problems with the plot.
- There are two dogs because I wanted Kazuki and Gouta to have to work together. Normally, I don't like for the good guys to outnumber the bad guys, and the dogs corrected the ratio. It's strange, but I don't have a problem with this when I'm watching shows like *Power Rangers*.
- The design was improvised. They may have been inspired a bit by Casshern's dog Friendar (from the old anime). I usually like to draw these kinds of things myself, but that's hard to do when you're on a weekly schedule, so my assistants did some of the panels. I wish I'd had the time to make them look and act more like real dogs.

KILLER RABIES

CHAPTER 61: WHO'S THE MONSTER?
DODDOM
TOKI-KO!!
RELAX! SHE ONLY GOT HIT SEVEN OR EIGHT TIMES.
SHE'S STILL ALIVE!
SHRSHHHHHHHHH
IF WE DEFEAT MARU-YAMA...
...HIS BUSO RENKIN WILL DEACTIVATE...
...AND TOKIKO SHOULD RETURN TO NORMAL!

WITH THESE WOUNDS, I'D BETTER NOT FIGHT YOU BOTH AT THE SAME TIME.
HUFF
HUFF
I'LL RETREAT FOR NOW.
!!
MARU-YAMA!!
BY THE WAY ...
YOU'D BETTER SEE TO YOUR LITTLE FRIEND.
SHE'LL MAKE A CRUNCHY TREAT FOR WILD DOGS OR FOXES.

DAMMIT!
MUTO, WHERE'S TOKIKO?!
I CAN'T FIND HER!
SKRSH
HHHHHH
I THINK THE WIND CARRIED HER AWAY!
LOOKS LIKE THE VALKYRIE SKIRT SHRANK WITH HER.
HOPEFULLY IT'LL BREAK HER FALL.
BUT MARUYAMA'S RIGHT...
AT THAT SIZE, SHE'S VULNERABLE TO PREDATORS.
A FIRST-AID KIT
A FIRST-AID KIT

CHAPTER 61: WHO'S THE MONSTER?

伸宏和月

READ THIS WAY
KSHHHHHH
HOO!
PLIP
HUFF
PLIP
HUFF
...
I WAS CARELESS.

BUT NEXT TIME...
...I'LL KICK HIS BUTT!
WELL ...
...THESE BANDAGES ARE BETTER THAN NOTHING.
KSHHHH
HMM...
I WAS WASHED DOWN-RIVER QUITE A WAYS.
TMP
I HAVE TO GET BACK TO KAZUKI AND GOUTA SOMEHOW...
OR AT LEAST CONTACT THEM.
NO. FIRST, I'D BETTER FIND SOME SHELTER. I DON'T WANT TO BE MISTAKEN...
...FOR A FIELD MOUSE.
SHWUSH
!

WAAAH!!
TOKI-KO?!
GO-ZEN?!
WELL, WELL...
WHUP

YOU'RE LOOKING A BIT THIN, TOKIKO.
!
PAPILLON!!
AND THOSE CLOTHES!
HAVE YOU NO SHAME?
THAT'S RICH, COMING FROM YOU!!
WHAT'S GOING ON HERE, GOZEN?! EXPLAIN!
AT LEAST YOUR ATTITUDE'S STILL BIG.
CALM DOWN, TOKIKO.
I'LL EXPLAIN.
BLEEP
!
OUKA?

NO SIGN OF HER OVER THERE.

YOU SEE ANYTHING?

HUFF

TMP

HUFF

HUFF

HUFF

NO-THING.

WHERE COULD SHE BE?!

!

VWRRB

BEEP

KAZUKI?

TOKIKO!

ARE YOU ALL RIGHT?

SORT OF.

...

SO I HEAR YOU'RE GOING TO TRANSFORM INTO A BRONZE-SKINNED MONSTER IN FIVE WEEKS.

SWUP

AH!

HEY!

YOU'RE HEAVIER THAN YOU LOOK.

I'M GOING TO HELP YOU, MUTO.

AND I EXPECT A LITTLE GRATITUDE.

YOU GUYS, GRAB WHAT YOU CAN OF OUR STUFF AND HEAD INTO TOWN!

WE'LL MANAGE WITHOUT YOU!

CHOUNO ...
IF ANY HARM COMES TO TOKIKO...
...YOU KNOW WHAT'LL HAPPEN.
DON'T BE INSULTING. I STOPPED PLAYING WITH DOLLS YEARS AGO.
NOW, IF SHE PROVOKES ME, THAT'S ANOTHER MATTER.

OH, THAT'S GREAT!!

BIRDS OF A FEATHER, HUH?!

WHUP

I'VE TRIED PUSHING REDIAL ON HIS CELL PHONE, BUT NO ONE ANSWERS.

IS TOKIKO ALL RIGHT?

HER SAFETY IS ALL THAT I CARE ABOUT!

I DON'T CARE IF HE GETS RE-EXTERMINATED OR BECOMES A MONSTER OR KILLS HIMSELF!

HMM...

HMM...

HMM...

TUP

!

GASP...

GASP...

GASP...

GASP...

GASP...

YOU MANAGED TO DEACTIVATE YOUR BUSO RENKIN BEFORE THEY KILLED YOU, HUH?
HMPH.

I'LL JUST TAKE THIS WITH ME.

YOU CAN'T REALLY COMPLAIN...
AFTER ALL, YOU DID TRY TO KILL US.
SMIRK

NO.
THERE'S NO NEED FOR THAT.
SWUP
THUD
ZAK
THE KAKUGANE WILL KEEP YOU ALIVE AND EVENTUALLY HEAL YOU.
ZAK
ZAK
ZAK
AND SOMEONE FROM THE ALCHEMIST ARMY WILL CERTAINLY COME FOR YOU.
DOOM
DON'T YOU...
...PITY ME!!

I'D RATHER DIE...
RASP
RASP
...THAN BE TREATED LIKE A DEFEATED DOG!
KILL ME!
NO.
WE USE OUR BUSO RENKIN TO KILL MONSTERS...
...NOT PEOPLE.
OUR POWER IS MEANT...
...TO PROTECT PEOPLE, REMEMBER?
GRK
BE-SIDES...
...UNDER DIFFERENT CIRCUMSTANCES, WE'D BE ON THE SAME SIDE.

INSTEAD OF FIGHTING EACH OTHER...

...WE'D BE FIGHTING THE REAL ENEMY.

TMP

LET'S GO, GOUTA.

HMPH...

ZAK ZAK

REMEM-BER THIS...

REMEM-BER THIS...

THE ALCHEMIST ARMY AND THE RE-EXTERMINATION SQUAD...

...EVEN TOKIKO AND I...

...WE ALL BELIEVE IN DESTROYING OUR ENEMIES.

WE BELIEVE IN THAT PHILOSOPHY COMPLETELY.

...WHO'S THE REAL MONSTER?

- Height: 165 cm; Weight: 55 kg
- Born: March 7; Pisces; Blood Type: A; Age: 20
- Likes: Toy dogs, picture books of dogs
- Dislikes: Real dogs
- Hobby: Watching talk shows
- Special Ability: Able to mimic various dog sounds
- Affiliations: Alchemist Army, Re-Extermination Squad

Character File No. 28

RINTARO INUKAI

Author's Notes

- I got the idea for the Buso Renkin of the Military Dogs first and developed Inukai's character to complement it. So basically, he only exists because of the Buso Renkin.
- Unfortunately, because he was created in a hurry, I really couldn't define his personality as much as I would have liked. But I kind of like creating characters that have something to prove.
- I based his design on one of the many character sketches I'd done previously. I especially like the sly smile and flippy hair.
- Try not to think of him as just a defeated dog. After all, you can't be defeated unless you have the courage to go into battle in the first place.

CHAPTER 62:

IKUSABE ATTACKS

Buso Renkin CHARACTER POPULARITY POLL!!

11th Place — Lotteriya Employee — 476 VOTES

12th Place — Homunculus Washio — 433 VOTES

13th Place — Homunculus Kinjo — 338 VOTES

14th Place — Buhiro Watsukino — 317 VOTES

15th Place — Victor — 289 VOTES

16th Place — Saa-chan — 278 VOTES

17th Place — Koji Rokumasu — 199 VOTES

18th Place — Chii-chin — 193 VOTES

19th Place — Bakushaku Chouno (Dr. Butterfly) — 116 VOTES

20th Place — Homunculus Jinnai — 50 VOTES

21st Place — Hideyuki Okakura — 48 VOTES

22nd Place — Jiro Chouno — 46 VOTES

22nd Place — St. Germaine Hospital Nurse — 46 VOTES

24th Place — Hayasaka Siblings' Mother — 44 VOTES

25th Place — Masashi Daihama — 42 VOTES

26th Place — Tai — 31 VOTES

27th Place — Doctor of St. Germaine Hospital — 25 VOTES

28th Place — Shinyo Suzuki — 24 VOTES

29th Place — Homunculus Hanabusa — 17 VOTES

30th Place — Newscasters — 13 VOTES

31st Place — Homunculus Kawazui — 12 VOTES

31st Place — The Men in Black — 12 VOTES

33rd Place — Homunculus Mita — 10 VOTES

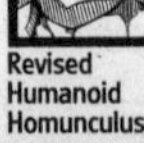

34th Place — Revised Humanoid Homunculus — 9 VOTES

35th Place — Reporter Oshikura — 8 VOTES

35th Place — Shi — 8 VOTES

37th Place — Homunculus Saruwatari — 7 VOTES

37th Place — Shishaku Chouno — 7 VOTES

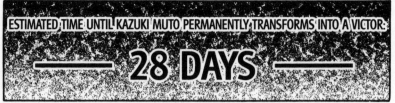

ESTIMATED TIME UNTIL KAZUKI MUTO PERMANENTLY TRANSFORMS INTO A VICTOR:

— 28 DAYS —

YAMASHITA PARK, YOKOHAMA CITY

BEEP

BEEP

BEEP

BEEP

BEEP

THE SUBSCRIBER YOU HAVE CALLED HAS THEIR PHONE TURNED OFF OR...

...IS CURRENTLY OUTSIDE THE COVERAGE AREA.

WHAT'S GOING ON? IT'S BEEN A WEEK...

WHY DON'T THEY PICK UP?!

DAMMIT!

BEEP

IS TOKIKO ALL RIGHT?

AND SHE'S NOT THE ONLY THING I'M WORRIED ABOUT...

963銀行
INUKAI...
...REALLY DID A NUMBER ON US.
WE MANAGED TO GET TO YOKOHAMA WITH THE MONEY WE HAD...
...BUT THERE ISN'T MUCH LEFT.
HEY!

I GOT US SOME SNACKS!
I WAS GOING TO SAY WE DON'T HAVE ANY MORE MONEY TO WASTE!

AW, MAN ...
I DON'T EVEN LIKE MOST OF THIS STUFF!
SORRY.
BUT...
...YOU KNOW WHAT THEY SAY. YOU CAN'T WAGE WAR ON AN EMPTY STOMACH.
IF YOU'RE SO HUNGRY ...
...WHY DON'T YOU JUST DO A LITTLE ENERGY DRAIN?

IF THAT'S A JOKE...

...IT'S NOT FUNNY.

...

HEY...

YEAH?

IF YOU MANAGE TO STOP YOURSELF FROM BECOMING A VICTOR...

WHAT DO YOU MEAN "IF"?

...ARE YOU STILL GOING TO BE AN ALCHEMIST WARRIOR?

WILL YOU BE ABLE TO FIGHT ALONGSIDE PEOPLE WHO TRIED TO KILL YOU?

...

I GUESS I CAN FIGHT ALONGSIDE ANYONE IF IT'S FOR A CAUSE I BELIEVE IN.

AS LONG AS WE'RE FIGHTING FOR THE SAME THING...
...WE CAN BE ALLIES.
!
VWRRRR
HELLO... WHO-
...
OH, GOOD. YOU'RE STILL ALIVE. ♡
PHONE
CHOUNO!
HEY! WHERE ARE YOU?!

横浜天飯
中華街
I'M IN CHINA-TOWN.
WHERE?
YOKO-HAMA.
MMM... THERE'S SOMETHING TO BE SAID...
...FOR EATING STEAMED PORK BUNS IN THE HEAT OF SUMMER. ♡
FORGET YOUR PORK BUNS!
HOW'S TOKIKO?!
TOKIKO?!

I'M FINE.
WELL, NOT ANY WORSE, AT LEAST.
HA
HA
OTHER THAN THE FACT THAT SHE'S WEARING BARBIE CLOTHES!
SHUT UP, PORK BUN HEAD!
WHAT DID YOU SAY?!
NO, YOUR HEAD'S A BEAN PASTE BUN!! IT'S FULL OF BEANS!!
HEY, DON'T TAKE IT OUT ON ME!
KEEN
SHE'S FINE.
YEAH.
WHY DIDN'T YOU CONTACT US SOONER?!
ANSWER ME!
MO WEASON.
JUS' DIDN'T FEEL LIKE IT.
I DON'T REALLY LIKE TO GET PHONE CALLS.
I LIKE MAKING THEM THOUGH. ♡
WHO IS THIS GUY?!
THAT'S JUST HOW HE IS.
CAN I HAVE THE PHONE?

CAN WE GET DOWN TO BUSINESS, CHOUNO?
I'M RUNNING OUT OF TIME.

HMPH...
FINE. WE'LL MEET TOMORROW MORNING...
...AT THE FOREIGNER'S CEMETERY.
ALL RIGHT.
AND THEN...
...WE'LL HEAD FOR NEWTON APPLE ACADEMY.

WHY AREN'T WE MEETING UP RIGHT AWAY?!

BECAUSE I'M GOING TO ENJOY SOME TASTY CHINESE FOOD TONIGHT.

YOU CAN'T WAGE WAR ON AN EMPTY STOMACH.
RIGHT?
KLAK
I AGREE.
IN YOUR CONDITION, GOING TO THAT RENDEZVOUS WOULD BE SUICIDE.

AT FIRST I THOUGHT YOU WERE JUST BEING CAPRICIOUS...
...BUT I'VE BEEN WATCHING YOUR EATING HABITS FOR A WEEK NOW.

YOU STARTED OUT AS AN INCOMPLETE HOMUNCULUS WITH AN INCURABLE DISEASE...
SINCE THE FINAL BATTLE WITH THE L.X.E., YOU'VE HEALED, BUT YOU STILL HAVEN'T COMPLETELY RECOVERED.

I'D SAY YOU'RE ONLY AT ABOUT 70 TO 80 PERCENT.
SMIRK
VERY OBSERVANT OF YOU.
YOU'RE SMARTER THAN I THOUGHT.
GACK

BUT I REALLY DO WANT SOME CHINESE FOOD.

SO MANY CHOICES ...♡

RAMEN! CHILI SHRIMP!

FINE. DO WHAT YOU WANT...

BUT REMEMBER...

I WON'T LET YOU EAT ANY PEOPLE.

I DON'T REQUIRE YOUR PERMISSION FOR THAT, BUT...

RIGHT NOW IT'S JUST CHINESE *FOOD* I'M CRAVING.

ALL RIGHT? ♡

!

BLEEP

STRANGE...

A HOMUNCULUS...

...WHO DOESN'T WANT TO EAT PEOPLE?

I'VE BEEN WONDERING ABOUT THAT AS WELL...

...IT SEEMS THAT PAPILLON'S DESIRE TO EAT PEOPLE HAS DIMINISHED.

AT LEAST, IN THE TWO WEEKS THAT I'VE BEEN WITH HIM, HE HASN'T SHOWN MUCH OF AN APPETITE FOR THEM.

WHAT?

FEEDING ON HUMAN BEINGS IS A PRIMAL INSTINCT FOR HOMUNCULI. WHEN HE FIRST TURNED, HE DEVOURED AT LEAST 20 PEOPLE.

WHAT'S GOING ON?

WHAT'S HAPPENING TO HIM?!

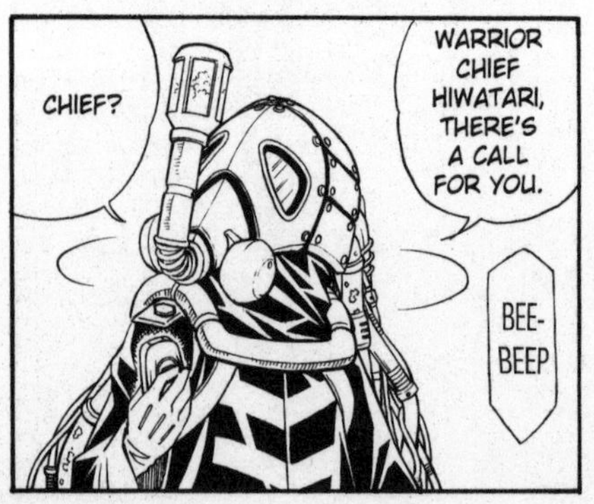

WARRIOR CHIEF HIWATARI, THERE'S A CALL FOR YOU.
CHIEF?
BEE-BEEP

Bath Room
ALL RIGHT. LET ME HAVE IT.
WHAM
KREKK
FSSSS
!!
SHUT UP, YOU. WHAT'S YOUR PROBLEM?
I... UM...
WHO IS IT?
CHITOSE.
WHERE?
PSHHK
NEWTON APPLE ACADEMY.
HAVING CROSS-REFERENCED WARRIOR BUSUJIMA'S RESEARCH...
...WITH MY OWN...
...I'VE CONCLUDED THAT THIS IS KAZUKI MUTO'S DESTINATION.

AND THE OTHERS?
NO SIGN OF THEM YET.
BUT IT'S BEEN A WEEK SINCE THE BATTLE IN OKUTAMA SO THEY MAY BE CLOSE.

I BELIEVE THEY'RE...

...WITHIN THE CITY LIMITS OF YOKOHAMA RIGHT NOW.

ALL RIGHT, CONTINUE YOUR MISSION.
YEAH?
OH... AND ANOTHER THING.
IS WARRIOR IKUSABE...
...WITH YOU RIGHT NOW?

READ THIS WAY

EVERY-BODY'S HERE...
...EXCEPT FOR BRAVO, THAT LOSER INUKAI, AND NEGORO—WHO'S PROBABLY IN HIDING.
THEN...
...GIVE HIM A MESSAGE FOR ME.
THE ITEM HE REQUESTED...
...ARRIVED THIS MORNING FROM HQ.

I'LL SEND YOU THE DETAILS.
GOOD-BYE.
KLIK

HEY WHAT'S THIS, SPECIAL TREATMENT?
WHATCHA GET?

MY LUNCH.
YOU CAN'T WAGE WAR ON AN EMPTY STOMACH.
THOOM
GOING OUT TO FIGHT?
YES.
TMP
YOKOHAMA'S A BIG CITY.
THAT'S OKAY. MY INSTINCTS HAVE NEVER LET ME DOWN.
KLAK

WARRIOR IKUSABE HAS DEFEATED MORE HOMUNCULI...
...THAN WARRIOR CHIEFS SAKIMORI OR HIWATARI.
HE'S VERY SURE OF HIMSELF.
IS HE THAT GOOD?
DON'T YOU KNOW?
IN FACT, OF ALL THE ACTIVE WARRIORS IN THE ALCHEMIST ARMY...
...HE CURRENTLY HOLDS THE RECORD FOR...
...THE MOST HOMUNCULI DESTROYED!!
NOW THEN...
WHERE SHALL I GO...
...FIRST?

Buso Renkin
ブソウレンキン

CHAPTER 63: GEKISEN, THE CROSS SPEAR
HMM?
中華街
THAT PRESENCE...
THERE'S A HOMUNCULUS NEARBY.
WELL...
MY INSTINCTS WERE LEADING ME SOMEWHERE ELSE...
BUT...
...HOW CAN I PASS THIS UP?
DOOM

YACK
YACK
HMM...
WHICH SHOP SHOULD I TRY?

THIS CROWD IS REALLY BOTHERSOME.

WELL, MAYBE IF YOU DIDN'T DRESS LIKE SUCH A FREAK, YOU WOULDN'T ATTRACT SO MUCH ATTENTION!

MY SENSE OF STYLE IS BEYOND YOUR TINY INTELLECT.
I PITY YOU.
YOU PITY ME?!
HEY, STOP TAKING PICTURES! WE'RE NOT SOME FREAK SHOW!

WHAT'S GOING ON?
YACK
YACK
THE CROWD'S PARTING...

CHAPTER 63:
GEKISEN, THE CROSS SPEAR

伸宏和月

WELL, WELL...

YOU'RE A SHARP DRESSER FOR A HOMUNCULUS.

IT SEEMS THAT NOT EVERYONE AMONG THE ALCHEMIST WARRIORS...

...LACKS AN APPRECIATION FOR *HAUTE COUTURE.*

HUH?
LOOKS LIKE MY INSTINCTS WEREN'T SO FAR OFF AFTER ALL.
IF YOU'RE TRAVELING WITH THIS GROUP...
...YOU MUST HAVE QUITE A STORY TO TELL, HOMUNCULUS.

SO I'LL ASK YOU ...
WHERE'S KAZUKI MUTO?
I KNOW WHERE HE IS...
BUT I'M NOT GONNA TELL YOU. ♡

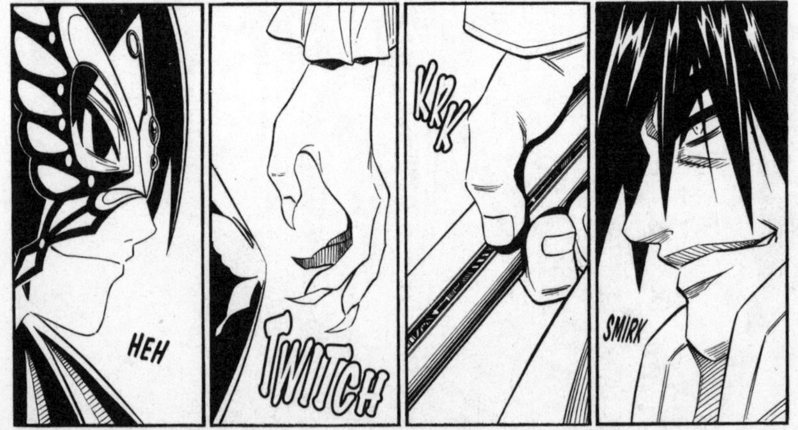

NO, YOU FOOL! YOU CAN'T FIGHT HERE!

YOU THINK YOUR FORMER COMRADE HERE WILL LET US GO?

DON'T BE NAIVE.

AND YOU!

YOU'RE AN ALCHEMIST WARRIOR! DON'T YOU KNOW BETTER THAN TO START A FIGHT IN THE MIDDLE OF CHINA-TOWN?!

HMM, I SUPPOSE YOU HAVE A POINT.

THERE'S AN ABANDONED WAREHOUSE DISTRICT A LITTLE WAYS FROM HERE.

WE CAN SLUG IT OUT THERE WITHOUT ANY INTERRUPTIONS.

LET'S DO IT!
AND MAKE ALL THE NOISE YOU WANT!

FLUTTER

...IT WON'T MATTER.

WHATEVER HE THROWS AT ME...

ZAK

BOOM

...I'LL BLOW AWAY...
...WITH MY NEAR-DEATH HAPPINESS.

TMP

SO YOU HAVE A BUSO RENKIN.
YOU'RE A REAL SPECIAL HOMUN-CULUS, EH?
BUT...
ZAK

THWOOM
?!
HEY!!
IT REPAIRED ITSELF!
AN ATTACK LIKE THAT...
...WON'T STOP GEKI-SEN!
RAPID AUTOMATIC RECOVERY!
THAT MUST BE THE CROSS SPEAR'S SPECIAL ABILITY!
SHOOOM

THEN ...
HOW ABOUT THIS?
BOOM
HIS ARM!
HE BLEW IT OFF!!

NOT GOOD ENOUGH!
ZAK ZAK ZAK
?!
SHING
SHING
WHAT ?!

THWAK
LIKE THAT?!

SO YOU HAVE THE POWER TO REGENERATE, EH?
WELL, LET'S SEE YOU REGENERATE FROM SMITHEREENS!
FWOOSH
BOO-BOO-BOOM

MAXIMUM ESCAPE VELOCITY!
WOOOOOOOO
ZAK
EEEEEEK!
PAPIL-
LON!
ARE YOU OUT OF YOUR MIND?!
TMP
OOPS. SORRY.
I HAVE A HARD TIME CONTROLLING MY STRENGTH WHEN I'M HUNGRY.
HUFF
HUFF

WOOOOOOO
WEEZ
WEEZ
PERHAPS THIS WAS A MISTAKE.
IF I'D TAKEN HIM ALIVE...
...WE COULD'VE QUESTIONED HIM ABOUT VICTOR AND THE ALCHEMIST ARMY.
HE'S TIRED.
IT'S NOT JUST THAT HE HASN'T FULLY RECUPERATED. HE WAS LIKE THIS WHEN HE FOUGHT KAZUKI, TOO. HE LACKS STAMINA BECAUSE HE'S NOT FULLY DEVELOPED.
I'VE FOUND PAPILLON'S WEAKNESS!
WHOA...
WHAT A MESS.
THERE'S NO TRACE ...
...OF HIM LEFT.

ZAK ZAK
?!!!
IMPOSSIBLE !!
SHING
SHING

THWOOOM
PHEW...
IT'S BEEN A WHILE SINCE I HAD TO DO A FULL BODY REGENER-ATION.
YOU HAVE A GREATER LIFE-FORCE THAN A HOMUNCULUS.
WHAT A PAIN.
VOLUME 7: RUNAWAY START
(THE END)

Liner Notes #55~60

Chapter 55: Rainy Emotions

- I'd been wanting to play around with Okakura's hair and thought that this would be a good time since we'll be leaving Ginsei Academy behind for a while. I almost gave up on the idea, having missed my opportunity after the final battle with the L.X.E., but I really enjoyed drawing this group.
- Gouta trips on a snail and falls. What a tragic character.
- The flashback sequence shows how Gouta fell for Tokiko, but I didn't want to do the usual "tragic past that made him what he is today" stuff. Instead, I showed how Tokiko motivated him to try to become strong for the future. You tend to remember the people who had an impact on you when you were in school. At least I do.
- The Re-Extermination Squad appears. The lack of pretty boys in this group triggered a massive booing from our female readers. I even got booed by Ms. Kurosaki.

Chapter 56: The New Third

- Gouta's fighting style and his Motor Gears are shown for the first time. I'm really glad I took some time to think about Gouta's attacks and how he would use the Motor Gears. I think this chapter turned out really well.
- The flames around Hiwatari were drawn by my assistants. They used Shishio's flames from *Rurouni Kenshin* for reference. This turned out to be more work than expected. Tones would have made the panels too busy so it had to be done the hard way. I got the idea for the flames coming out of Hiwatari's mouth from the American comic book character Chamber from *Generation X*. Sorry if I played around too much.
- Gouta joins forces with Tokiko and Kazuki. Once again we have a fighting threesome. Then again, I thought that enough time had passed that the readers may have forgotten this recurrent motif. I like to set up new encounters in places where a loss occurred.

Chapter 57: Runaway Start

- Gouta is willing to join them, but he won't shake hands with Kazuki. I decided to make the snub more comical than serious.
- Chitose calls Bravo on the phone. She says that she can hear in his voice that his heart isn't in killing Kazuki. When I wrote those lines, I thought I was being very clever because you can't hear voice tones in manga!
- My favorite scene in this chapter is the three of them under one umbrella. Tokiko invites Kazuki to come out of the rain, and Gouta invites himself. Then Kazuki casually tilts the umbrella toward Gouta so he doesn't get wet. I really like the way each character was portrayed here. Situations like this don't usually happen in a boy's comic.
- The readers are starting to think of Papillon as comic relief, but I've always considered him to be the anti-hero of the story. And I really work hard so that his lines sound cool...or so I thought.

Chapter 58: Episode Zero

- Using locales like Asakusa, Okutama, and Yokohama to create a sense of travel didn't work as well as I'd hoped. It's hard to do a "road movie" in a weekly comic.
- Taking a leak together is one of the things men just do. I've always wanted to show a scene like this. Gouta steals a peek, which shows that he has the weaker will. And the fact that Kazuki doesn't care shows his self-confidence. That's why Gouta gets labeled as the Underdog.
- Newton Apple. I really like this name. I like the "gravity" those words seem to have. And some say that Newton was an Alchemist. I had to go with this name for the school.
- The appearance of the mysterious masked figure. The mask was inspired by the movie *Vidocq*. It's a French film like *Brotherhood of the Wolf* (where I got the idea for the Silver Skin). I thought that nobody would catch on because *Vidocq* is a more obscure film, but I was mistaken. Combine that with Chamber from the previous chapters and I may be losing my touch. I'll be sure to be more careful.

Chapter 59: No Intention of Losing

- First of all, let's not ask questions like "where did Kazuki come from?" Kazuki appears out of the sky and he seems very calm and collected. A man who's made up his mind is a very cool thing.
- The Bubble Cage makes its appearance. I wish I could have made the bubbles bursting out of Maruyama like guts, but the deadline was upon us before I could get my assistants to understand what I wanted. All I could do was swallow my tears. The shot of Tokiko and Gouta coming out of the holes they'd dug beside the tents didn't come off very clearly either. And neither did the deactivation of the Killer Rabies. This chapter was full of little disappointments.
- Maruyama appears. To counter the booing female fans, as well as Ms. Kurosaki, I made the man inside the suit good-looking...only he turned out to be a bit light in the loafers. It's no good, I just can't seem to draw pretty boys anymore.

Chapter 60: Wind and Leaves

- Inukai went on too long about the special abilities of the Killer Rabies. I know that long speeches bore the readers but with the number of pages I had to work with, it couldn't be helped. Every chapter seems to be a struggle because I have to tell so many stories but I don't want the characters to be too flat.
- Tokiko vs. Maruyama. I finally got to show Tokiko enclosed in a cage of balloons, hence the name of the weapon. But, overall, it didn't work out as well as I'd hoped.
- Kazuki and Gouta's fight scenes were a lot of fun to draw. We didn't have much time to plan out the fights, but their fear that Tokiko is in trouble is very visible in their expressions. It's rare for people to be able to work together so well without talking. I think one should treasure such friends.
- Tokiko is miniaturized in battle. I used her clothes and small items to show how small she'd become, but this trick created a whole new batch of problems for me in the next chapter.

Chapter 61: Who's the Monster?

- Oh, no! Tokiko is going to be naked from this point on! What should I do?! And from that point on, I had to scramble for ideas. Ever since the chapters with the swimsuits, I've become more comfortable drawing the female form, but naked is a bit too much. Anyway, this is a manga for young boys. So, Ms. Kurosaki and I thought long and hard about how to get out of this situation. Then she said, "Well, she did bandage the boys' hands," and I thought, "That's it!" and ended up using up too many pages to show how Tokiko got out of that situation.
- Tokiko meets up with Papillon. The main point of this chapter was to make Kazuki and Gouta work together, and to put Tokiko with Papillon. The comment Papillon makes about being too old to play with dolls is really about me. Sure, my dolls tend to be collectible action figures, monsters, and robots, but, well…
- The line "who's the real monster" is the main theme of an upcoming storyline. Also, up until this point, Gouta only cared about Tokiko, but here he starts to admire Kazuki. It's an important turning point.
- Inukai gets beaten like the dog he is. If only I'd had more pages to work with him…

Chapter 62: Ikusabe Attacks

- The big issue at hand here was the popularity poll. What battle manga has a female character get the most votes? I guess I achieved one of my goals by creating a leading female character that fights, but, actually, there was one fan that sent in a large number of votes for Tokiko. Otherwise, Kazuki would have come in first.
- Inukai was so pathetic that I decided to allow him a small victory–he tore up their money. It might not seem very important in a boy's comic, but in the real world, not having money is a serious problem.
- The relationship between Kazuki and Gouta continues to improve a little. The trouble is, as long as Tokiko exists, the two can never really be friends.
- Since they were in Chinatown, I put Tokiko in a Chinese dress. Girls have to be fashionable, right? I'll have to explain what Chitose was doing in a schoolgirl uniform at a later date. Sorry.
- Papillon's lessening appetite for people is something I've been working on since the start. The question is, how will a person who's not completely a Homunculus but no longer human behave?
- Papillon's line about not liking to receive calls but liking to make them is another example of my personal habits being transferred to my characters. I guess I'm a lot like Papillon–we're both a little twisted.

Chapter 63: Gekisen, the Cross Spear

- The line where Ikusabe compliments Papillon's outfit shows that Ikusabe isn't quite right in the head. Have I become incapable of creating a normal character?
- I got the idea for Gekisen's special abilities from watching *Hollow Man*. I had to study up a bit on muscles and bones, but it was fun to draw. Still, I think I need to study some figure drawing in the future to get the muscles right.
- This chapter was a bit thin for Buso Renkin, but the impact of the Cross Spear's power seems to have saved it. Anyway, it was worthwhile because it may have given me an idea for a later storyline. That was a nice turn of events.

- And so → To be continued. 和月伸宏

Buso Renkin
ブソウレンキン

Coming Next Volume

Kazuki and Tokiko are still on the run! They head toward Apple Newton Academy, the place where Tokiko originally retrieved Kazuki's black kakugane. Tokiko is reduced to the size of a doll, but she still manages to fight alongside Kazuki and Gouta to take on three of the hunters and Captain Bravo himself! All this, plus the story of Captain Bravo's past revealed!

Available Now!

SJ ADVANCED
EYESHIELD 21™
Gear up for the best bone-crushing slapstick football manga ever!
Manga on sale now!
$7.99
EYESHIELD 21
SHONEN JUMP ADVANCED
Story by RIICHIRO INAGAKI
Art by YUSUKE MURATA
SHONEN JUMP ADVANCED
On sale at:
www.shonenjump.com
Also available at your local bookstore and comic store.
RATED T+ FOR OLDER TEEN
viz media
www.viz.com

SUBSCRIBE TODAY & BECOME A MEMBER OF THE SHONEN JUMP SUBSCRIBER CLUB...
You'll get:
*Access to Exclusive Online Content!
*50% Savings Off the Newsstand Price!
*Exclusive Premiums!
All this available ONLY to Subscribers!
SHONEN JUMP
THE WORLD'S MOST POPULAR MANGA ™
FILL OUT THE SUBSCRIPTION CARD ON THE OTHER SIDE, OR SUBSCRIBE ONLINE AT:
www.shonenjump.com